NATIONAL GEOGRAPHIC

D0602846

What Is the Pattern?

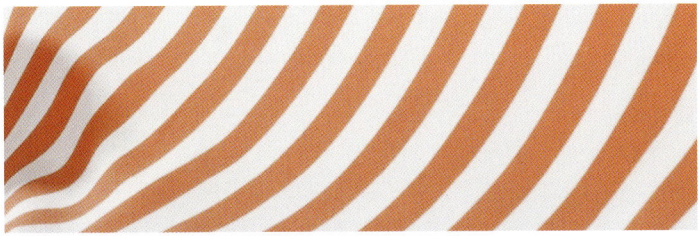

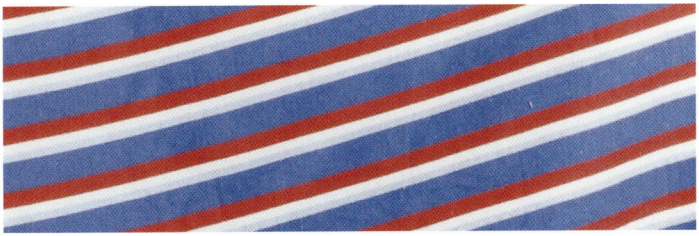

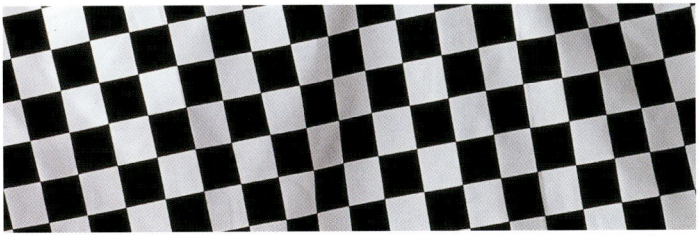

Jan Pritchett

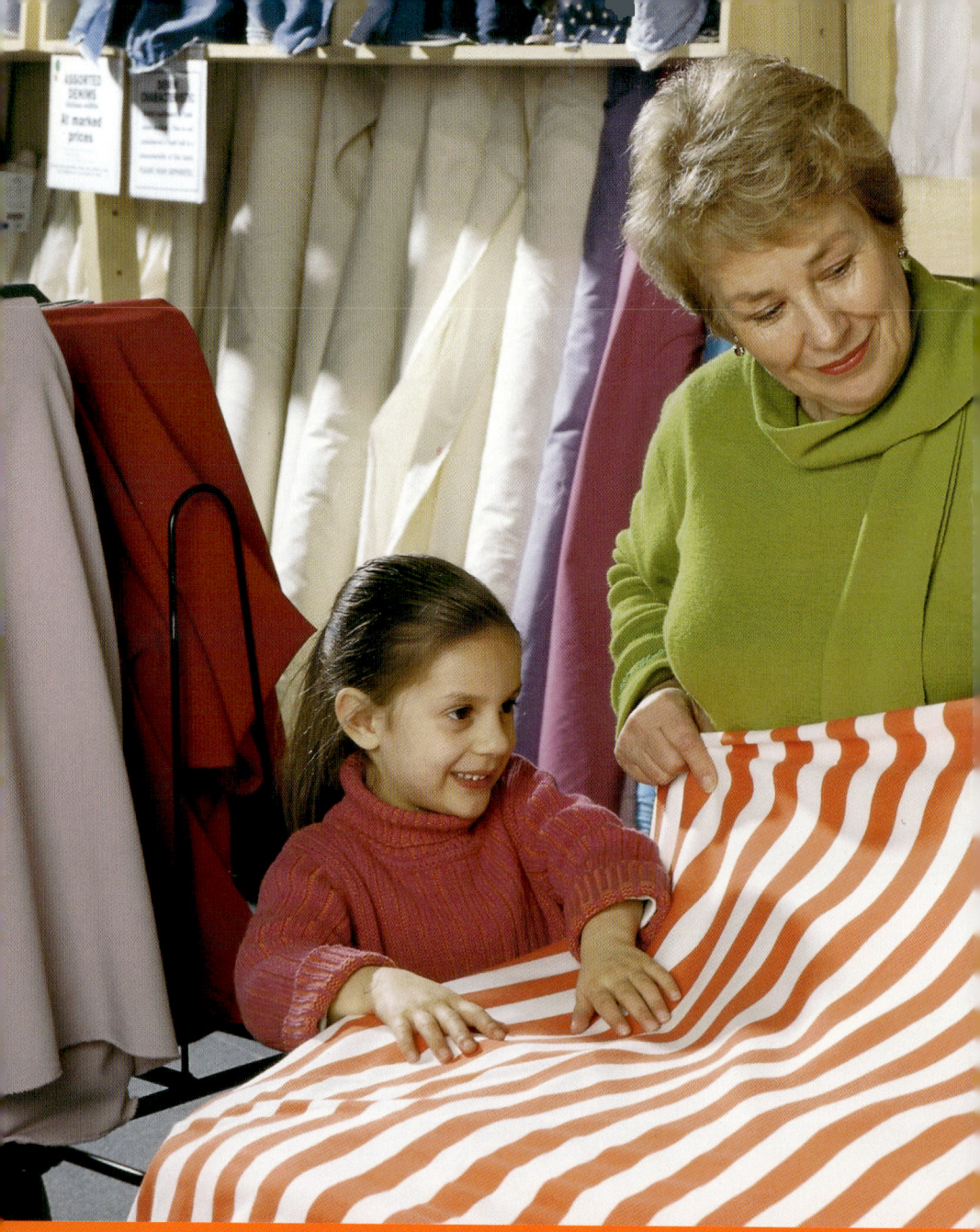

2 What is the pattern?

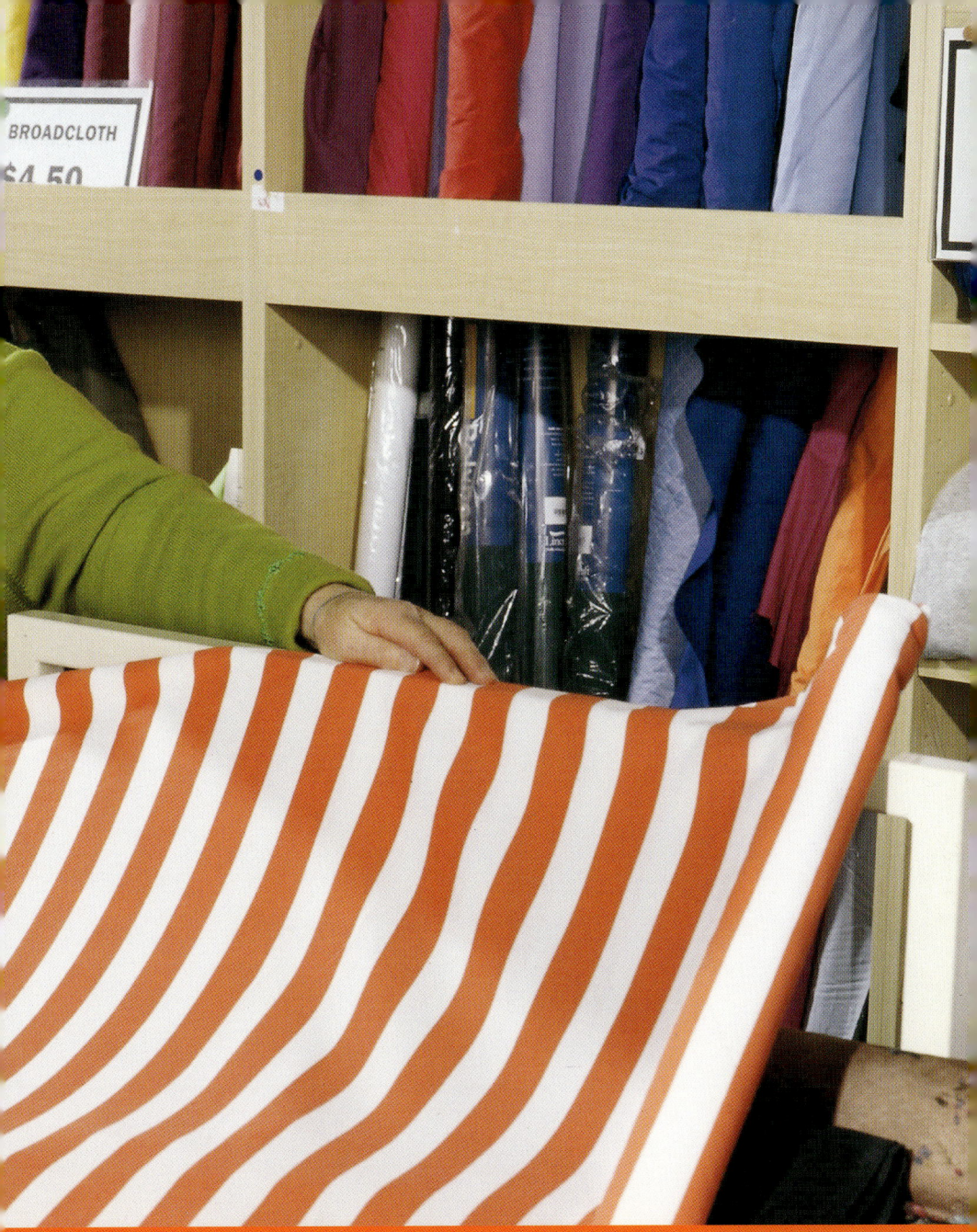
BROADCLOTH

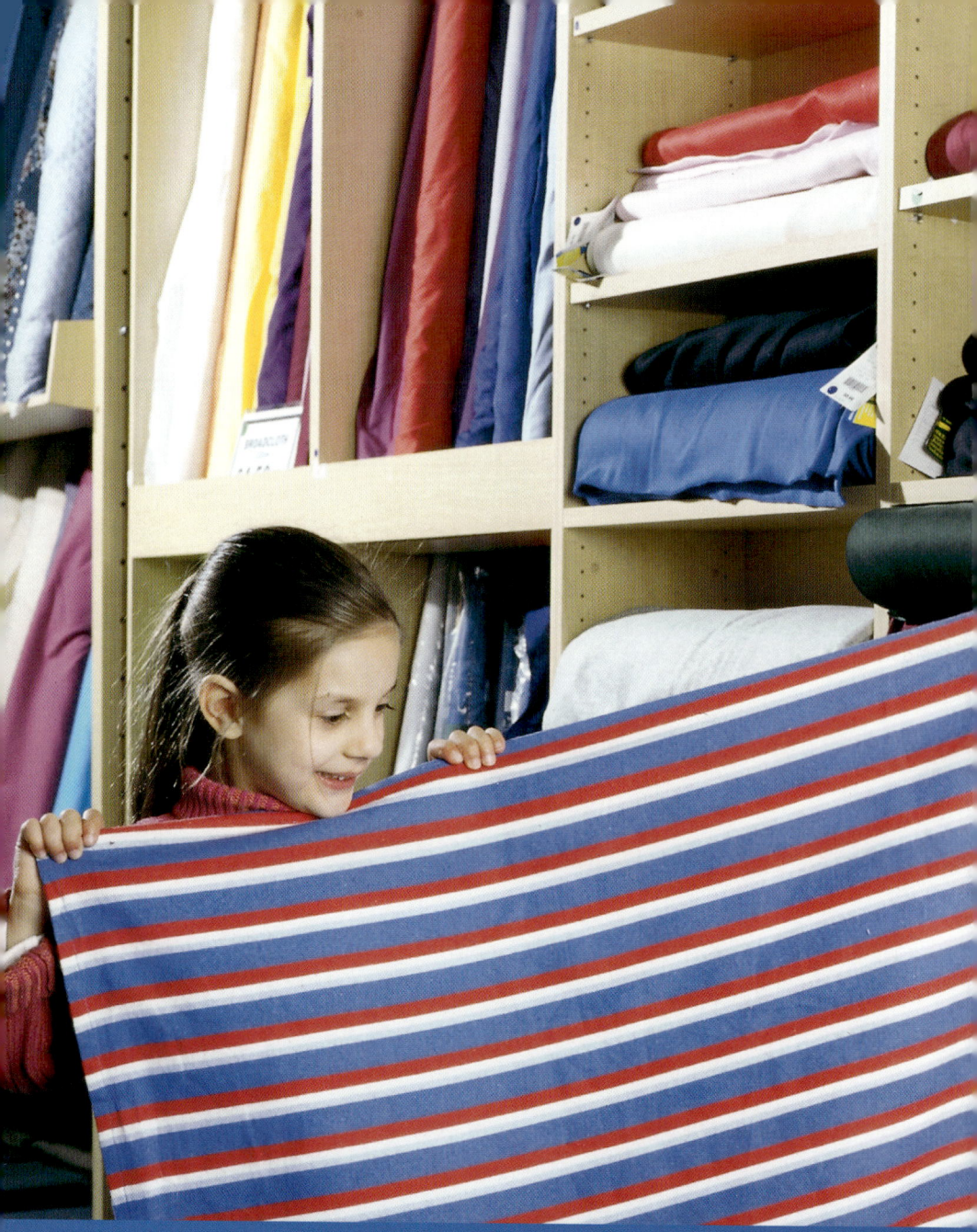

4 What is the pattern?

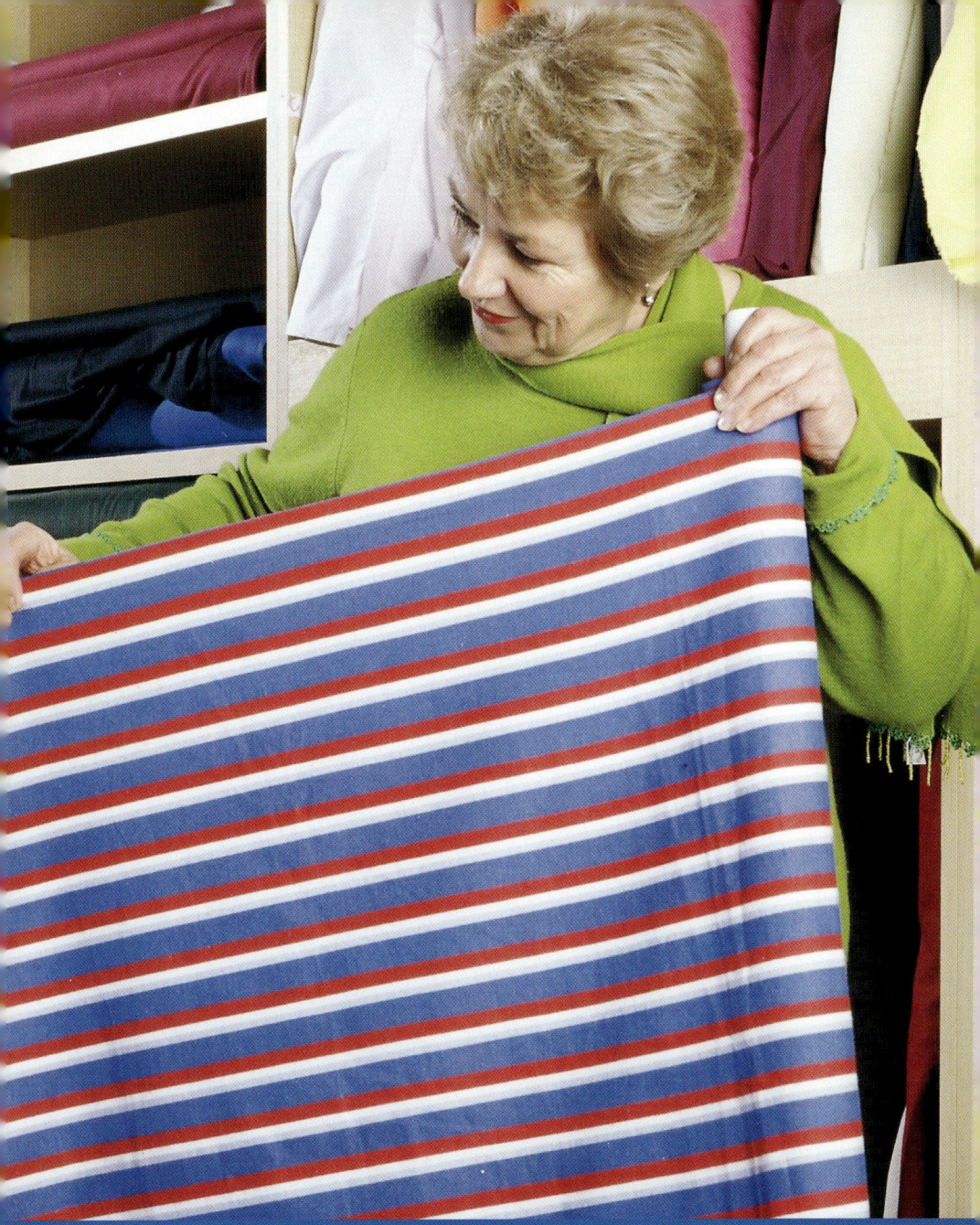

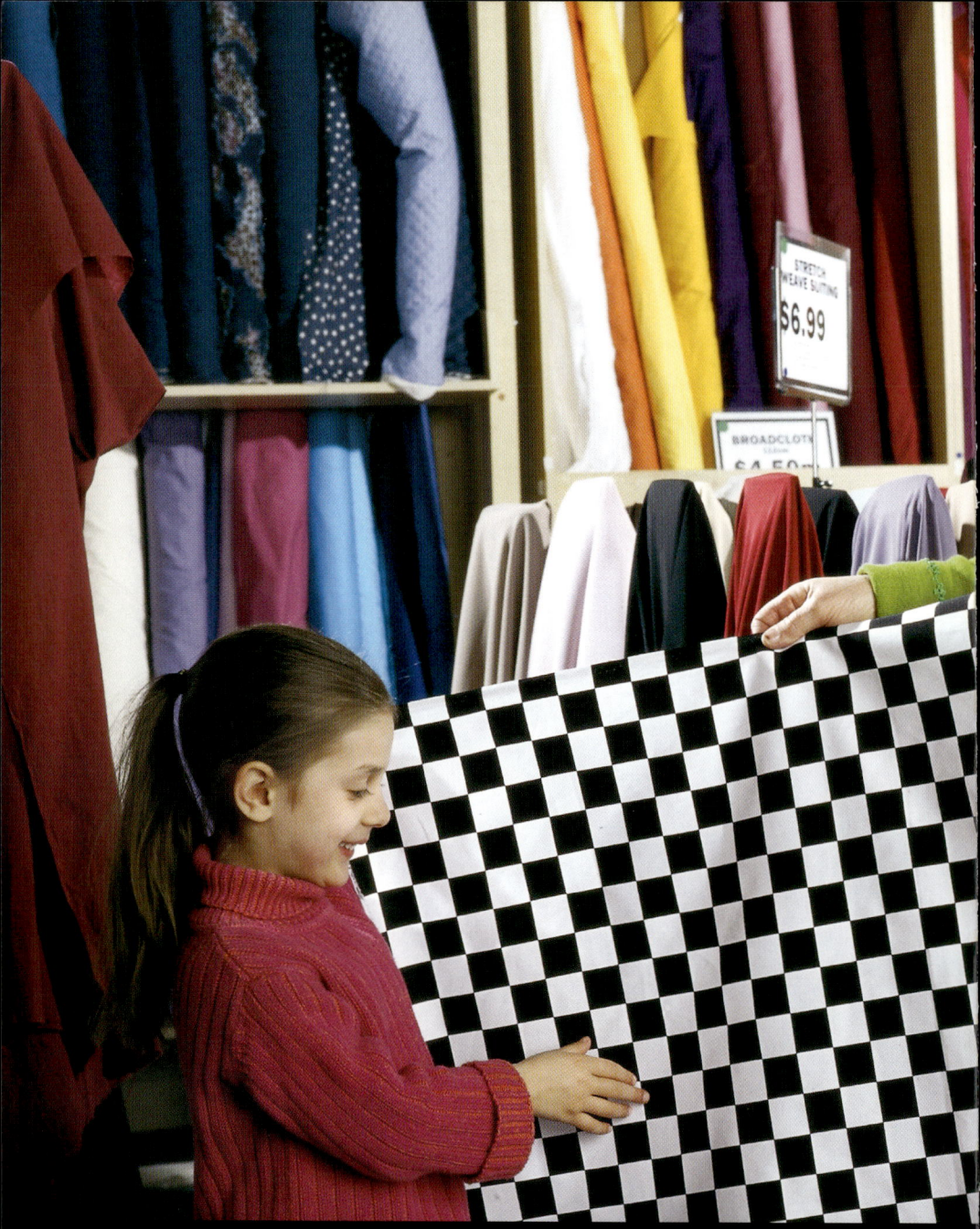

6 What is the pattern?

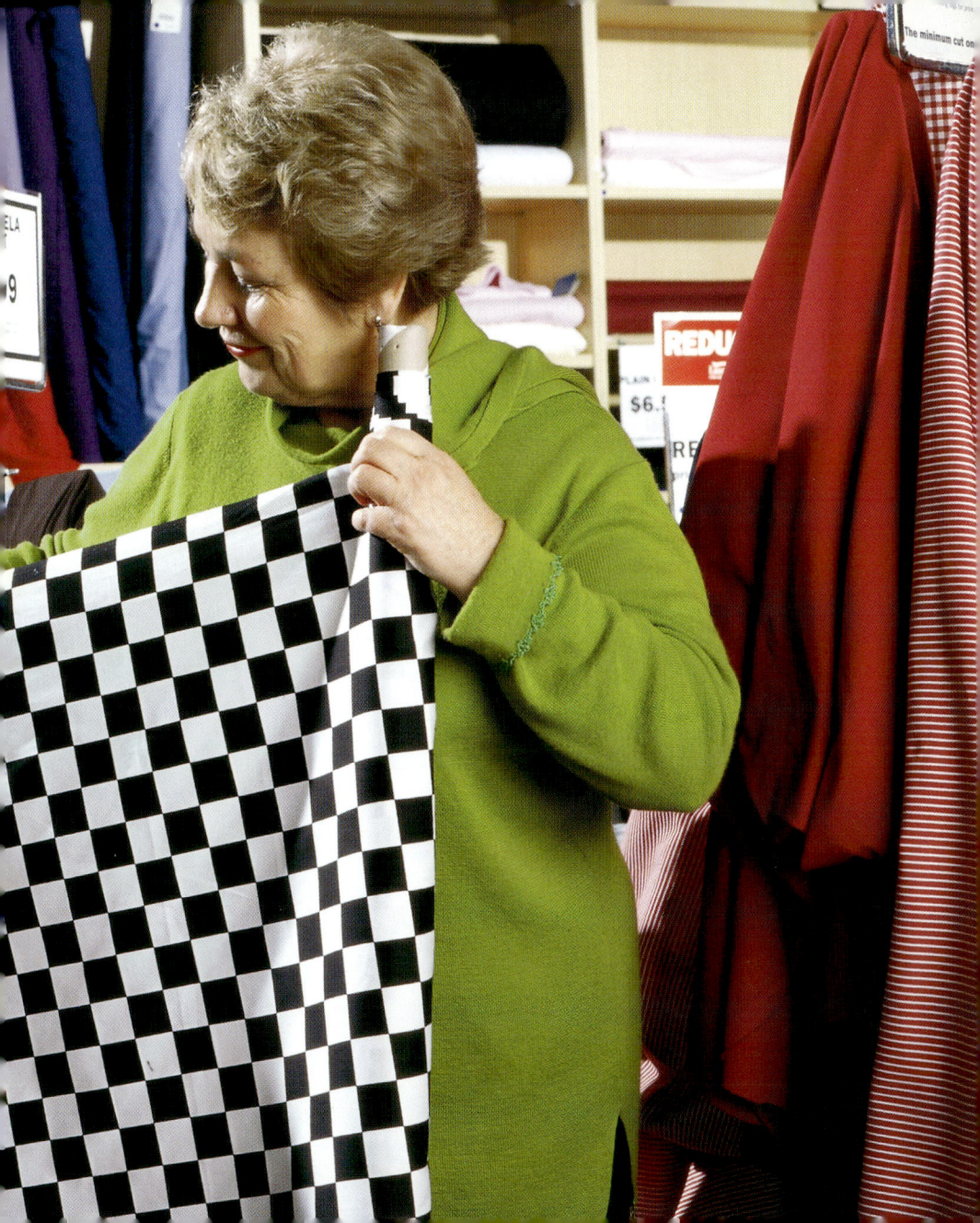
The minimum cut on
REDU
$6.

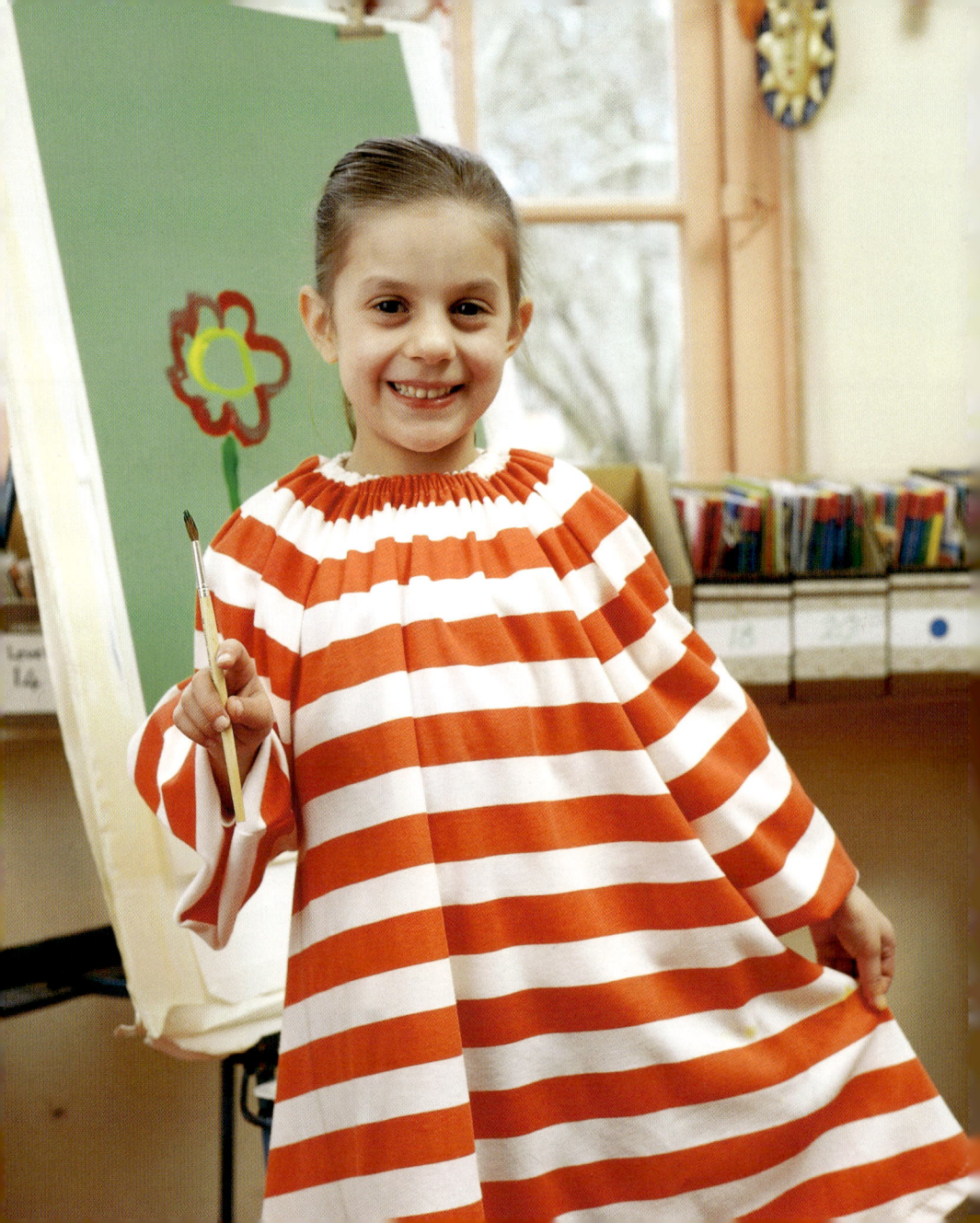